Be Beautiful Personally:
Single Is the New Sexxy

Keedra A. Keeley

Front and Back Cover Illustration by

I Will Be Beautiful & 225 Designs

Copyright © 2016 by Keedra A. Keeley & I Will Be Beautiful, LLC

ISBN-13: 978-0692646403 (Be Beautiful)
ISBN-10: 069264540X

Published By: Keedra A. Keeley and I Will Be Beautiful, Inc.
Atlanta, GA

Printed in the United States of America

All rights reserved. No part of this book may be reproduced, stored in retrieval systems, or transmitted in any form, by any means, including mechanical, electronic, photocopying, recording or otherwise, without prior written permission of the publisher.

• DEDICATION •

This book is dedicated to my best friends Monet, Andrea, and Erica, and my cousin Keesha, who are all more like sisters. I love you ladies and thank you so much for all of the years you have provided me with your sisterhood and love. Our day is coming when we will be able to celebrate each other's love together!

Until then, stay *Sexxy*!!

• Contents •

SECTION ONE

From The Author	7
How to Use This Book	12
Defining Beauty	14

SECTION TWO

Week 1: The Art of Being Single	20
Week 2: A Focused Woman is a Sexxy Woman	36
Week 3: A Secure Woman is a Sexxy Woman	55
Wek 4: A Praying Woman is a Sexxy Woman	71
Bonus Chapter: Every Man Isn't Ready for a Wife	87

SECTION THREE

Appendix	95

SECTION one

• FROM THE AUTHOR •

First let me start off by saying I do not claim to be a relationship expert! I can however say I am an expert at being a woman, because I am one, and I am an expert at living this single life, because I have had to learn how to be happy with myself without a relationship. So Single is the New Sexxy is not to give any woman advice on a relationship; when I am finally in one that is healthy and consistent, I promise to write a book about it. This book is about what I know best, learning how to create a life I love living and not depending on a man or a relationship to make me happy.

If I had to choose a major in the University of Life, it would definitely be Single! I swear I can do this single thing with my eyes closed, hands tied behind my back, and feet bound together. By choice of course, because I could settle for a crappy relationship for the sake of having a man. Yes, just like every other woman, or almost every other woman, I want a successful relationship. But life just hasn't swung its favor toward me when it comes to a successful, committed, and consistent relationship. And yes, sometimes, I really want to scream out of frustration. Well, all the time I want to scream out of frustration. Especially at this stage in my life, when I am achieving accomplishments and want to share them with a companion. Or when I get invited to events and want a hot sexxy date. Or when I come home after a long day and want to cuddle up next to someone to get a recharge. Or even on the holidays and birthdays when everyone else are sharing pictures on Facebook and Instagram with them and bae in their coordinated outfits, showing all of us how ridiculously happy they are, and making us single folks green with envy when they post pics captioned "She said YES?" or "He asked, I said YES!" Or when I just want a human diary to share everything about me with. Don't get me wrong, I am happy and very excited for all of my friends and family who seem to have more success in relationships and marriages than I seem to do with getting in the suggested daily intake of water each day. But I had to make a decision for myself, and that was if I just had to live this life single I might as well do it feeling and being sexxy!

    I have a lot of friends who are married, have children, or married with children. Aside from my best friends who do not live near me, the friends that were close to me were never available because they were either with their man or husband, busy being a mom, or doing both with their families. So I found myself spending a lot of time alone. When I finished college, I moved away from my college roommate Rachelle, who I used to go to every single club with almost every single day of the week (fun times). That is when I found myself no longer wanting to hang out all night. But because most of my friends and family were preoccupied and I didn't have any single friends, this made for some very lonely times. I started to feel like people were judging me because by the age of 25 I didn't have a husband, any children, or wasn't even in a relationship. People didn't take me seriously and thought I was immature and wasn't serious about my life. While this made me angry, I began to internalize these things and felt as though it was a man and a relationship that I needed to fill this void and no longer feel inadequate. And so that's what I went after, with not much success. Relationship after relationship failed. One was with a man who was still legally married but separated from his wife. Another wasn't even a relationship, it was, ya know, my boo…who I saw regularly….at night. He was much older than me and I called him my old man. Then I settled for a relationship where he had so many secrets and eventually moved to another state. We tried the long distance thing for a while but because I just couldn't take the secrets, it ended. And lastly, there was the one where I was just plain ole insecure, from the beginning to the very end. Oh man did I beg him something serious not to break off our relationship.

I felt there was so much pressure to either be in an ideal committed relationship, be married, or be married with kids. And not so much from my family, but from my social circles, in particular the church. So much so, I found myself competing with other women to have that ideal relationship or marriage. And I noticed other women competing with other women in the same way. We all wanted to be a good man's wife, and we all wanted other women to look at us with envy because of it.

What I experienced as a single woman in church was that we were treated differently than women who were categorized as one of the three I mentioned. We were chosen over the married women to work tirelessly within the church. We were asked constantly about our relationship status and when it would change. We were constantly asked about our relationships, as if it were a barometer to see if anything has changed or progressed to what may seem like a soon to come proposal. It felt like our voices weren't heard and we weren't paid as much attention to as the married women. It felt like we were shunned to the side as if our lives and accomplishments weren't as important as a marriage. And it almost seemed like we were looked upon as if to say "what is wrong with her" or "she must be fast" because we actually dated a few people hoping one of them would want a serious relationship. Oh and don't let us single women come around the married women's husbands or the seriously committed boyfriend. It was almost like an electric fence went up and if you came anywhere near him the look that was given was you will get electrocuted. Man, being a single woman, it's tough. I get it!

Now that's not to say I am not genuinely happy for my friends who have found love. I'm not saying that at all. But I just want every married woman, every engaged woman, every woman in a seriously committed relationship, and every single woman to know: THERE IS NOTHING WRONG WITH BEING SINGLE. It doesn't always mean you're a "hoe", it doesn't always mean you shouldn't or can't be taken seriously, it doesn't always mean you have all this extra time to just be working tirelessly because you don't have to go home to cook a man's dinner. Sometimes, a woman is single because she chooses to be, isn't trying to be in a crappy unhealthy and unhappy relationship, or is more focused on getting her life together than getting together with someone else. Don't forget committed women, you were once single too!

It wasn't until after much heartache, a flood of what seemed to be never ending tears, and even the thought of no longer wanting to live this life alone (for like the 6th and last time) I changed my focus. I changed my focus to me. I made my life all about me and only me. Now I know that sounds conceited and selfish, and I was called both, but trust me it wasn't. I focused on who I was, what I was, why I was, and all of the ways that I could fulfill those things to find a place of being happy without a man by my side and without the need to be in a relationship. I had to forgive myself for thinking me alone was not good enough and that I needed someone else to bring or give me fulfillment.

I know, sexxy is typically spelled with one "x" and not two. That is because this sexxy has nothing to do with sex, and everything to do with a woman being healthy and stable mentally, emotionally, spiritually, physically, and personally, which is what I call the Beauty Code. It's a new type of sexxy. When a woman has herself together in these five areas, and lives by The Beauty Code, there is nothing more attractive and more sexxy. Since I have had so much time spent with a single status listed on Facebook, I have become an expert on how to live as a single Black woman.

This book is a snippet of the journey I took to find happiness and Beauty in my single status. Single is the New Sexxy is not to teach women how to get a man, or even how to be single and satisfied. It's about women using their single status to empower themselves to be better, greater, and more beautiful in the way they think, in their emotional stability, in their spiritual strength, in their physical health, and in their own personal relationship with themselves. This book is about you, and making you the main priority and the main focus in your life. Single is the New Sexxy will help women realize that to be single is to first achieve wholeness as a woman, and in this wholeness everything else in life is achieved, accomplished, and attained.

I Will Be Beautiful is all about helping women find healing in their hurting places. I found that my hurting places left me feeling like tarnished goods. When I was at that point in my life I didn't feel good about myself and it was hard for me to find reasons to love myself. Once I pushed through that I arrived at a place where I felt Beautiful not only on the outside, but on the inside as well. The place where it truly matters.

I wish I could give you more at one time, but to keep it within the 30 days, I'm starting you off with the most important lessons I've learned on how to be single and fulfilled all at the same time, while reaching a whole new level of sexxiness within myself! With every book, I hope you enjoy, and I hope you find these things helpful to your own life, your own happiness, and your own healing. There is nothing more sexxy than a woman who knows herself, loves herself, appreciates herself, values herself, and finds the Beauty within herself. If you don't take anything else away from this book, I hope that is the one thing that is made clear! Enjoy your journey!

• How to Use This Book •

The *Be Beautiful* book series is comprised of a series of 30 day work books for women. Each book is focused on one of the five *Beauty* Codes. Each week there is a different subject and I share my own personal story around that subject. Once you have read my story, each day of the week you are then charged with an area of reflection that will take you on the journey of processing and working through your own personal story. In order to get the full intent of the book, **you must stay dedicated to doing the work each day.**

At the end of my personal narrative I have included Post-It Notes with a few poignant points. If you were to come to my house, you would see Post-It Notes all over the place as little reminders and sources of daily encouragement. So my suggestion to you is to either use the points that are highlighted on the Post-It Notes I provided as a starting point and/or pick your own and post them up anywhere in your house you will see them frequently.

Lastly, have fun! This is meant to help you grow through self-reflection, but it is also meant for you to have fun with getting to know yourself! And know that you are worth every single second you spend on yourself!

• DEFINING BEAUTY •

If I asked you to write down words that described beauty, what would you write? How would you define or describe beauty? Then I would ask who informed you that these descriptions and definitions represented beauty? Western society has given us a standard of beauty: small waist, long hair, straight hair, for skin tones that contain melanin the lighter the skin the more beautiful, white skin tones, full eyelashes, and light colored eyes. Unfortunately, women draw their self-esteem from these standards of beauty that are fed to us.

But there are many forms of Beauty as it pertains to a woman. Mentally, Emotionally, Spiritually, Physically, and Personally are, to me, all the components that make a woman whole and complete. It is in these five components that I have come to define true Beauty.

To Be Beautiful Mentally is a mentality. It is to be mentally strong and stable, to be a positive thinker, and to have healthy thoughts toward one's own self. Our thoughts are very powerful and they have the ability to dictate everything about ourselves and our lives. If the Bible is your choice of spiritual inspiration and empowerment, Philippians 4:8 gives a guide as to how we should conduct our thoughts and that is on good things. When we fail to have a strong, powerful, and healthy mentality we fail to honor who, what, and why we are as women.

To Be Beautiful Emotionally is to be emotionally stable. As women, we tend to be very emotional. It is ok to have emotions, it is a good thing and a sign that you are human. It is when we let our emotions cloud our judgement and cause us to acted rationally that our emotions are not healthy. When we act on impulse based on our emotional state instead of experiencing our emotions, riding out the emotional wave, and *then* deciding on a course of action, we fail to honor who, what, and why we are as women.

To Be Beautiful Spiritually is to be connected to your inner spirit. This is obtained through prayer, meditation, and personal reflection. Being and staying connected to the spiritual power that works inside of you is essential for obtaining success in all other Be Beautiful target areas. It creates balance, tranquility, peace, and understanding, that's why it falls in the middle of all the target areas. When we are lost and can't find a sense of peace within ourselves, is when our spiritual nature needs to be nurtured. As women, our roles and contributions to human existence are vital, so it is important that we are first plugged in to spirit. When we fail to actively and consistently nurture our spirit, we fail to honor who, what, and why we are as women.

To Be Beautiful Physically is to love and appreciate the natural skin you are in, and living a healthy lifestyle. This includes Black women loving their skin tones and complexions whether it is light skin, brown skin, dark skin, or mixed skin. It includes embracing your natural hair texture. It includes embracing your natural physical features. It includes embracing a healthy lifestyle in order to take care of your temple. It includes knowing your Beauty is not defined by your body type and size, but keeping healthiness as an obtainable goal. It is understanding what a woman's body is created for, and using it responsibly. When we fail to embrace our physical selves just the way we are then we fail to honor who, what, and why we are as women.

To Be Beautiful Personally is to know who you are, what you are, and why you are. As women, we play many different roles, to many different people, at many different times. So making sure to take the time out for yourself for self-care, to connect with yourself, and to love on yourself allows you to learn how to love yourself first. Loving on yourself is essential to Being Beautiful because just as the saying goes, if you don't love you, how you can you expect anyone else to love you, or how you can expect to know how to love anyone else. When we fail to explore who we really are and learn to love on ourselves, then we fail to honor who, what, and why we are as women.

Be Beautiful! It's Your Right!

SECTION TWO

I hated being single. OMG! I hated it!! I wanted someone to love me, I wanted someone to love, and I wanted that companionship that a relationship offers. I saw everyone around me who were either in what appeared to be healthy relationships with the love of their life or happily married, and wanted that for myself. I wanted Friday night date night, I wanted to spend my holidays with someone, I wanted a valentine, I wanted a birthday date, and most of all I did not want to be or feel lonely any longer. I wanted a man and I wanted him now! I felt that God had forgotten about me and I would wonder what was wrong with me. Did I do something to make God mad at me and this was my punishment? Was I too picky? Were all of the good men taken? For the life of me I could not figure out what the issue was and it was driving me insane! I was crying all the time, I would get mad at God and tell God we weren't cool until my prayers were answered, and I even told God that I was NOT going to continue doing what I was being called to do if I was not blessed with a husband. I threw the ultimate tantrum an adult woman could possibly throw. Yet, nothing changed. Just crappy, unhealthy, non-progressive relationships.

Does any of this sound familiar? Have you gone through these tantrums yourself? Well, I would venture out and guess yes, this sounds very familiar to you and yes you have gone through these same tantrums. When I sit and talk with other women, I hear in them the same things that I was going through, the same feelings I was experiencing and the same frustration I was feeling. So please believe me when I say, there is hope on this yellow brick road and it does lead to somewhere. Maybe not to Oz, but definitely a happy, single, and mentally peaceful place.

Well, my desires haven't changed. I still want the husband, holidays, birthdays, companionship, date nights, and all of that. But I am no longer spending countless hours and tears agonizing over when it all arrives. I won't lie, sometimes the road does get a little difficult when you want someone there with you during certain times and events in your life. But because I do not want to settle for just anything and anyone for the sake of filling an open slot, I have managed the art of being single. I call it an art because not everyone knows how to be unmarried and unattached while at the same time maintaining happiness. For most people, it really is something they have to work on and be intentional about. Some people depend their whole lives on having a companion. But it takes having to shift your views and perceptions of what being single really means.

So let's start there. Let's explore a new meaning within ourselves of what being single really is. I'll tell you what worked for me, I changed my view from being single and lonely to being the creator of my personal sacred space and my destiny. I took the time to really invest in myself by getting to know everything I possibly could about me. I like peace and tranquility, it is what keeps me balanced. So I had to learn how to create that around me when I couldn't make it to my most peaceful and tranquil place, the beach. In my audio book, A Single Gurl's Survival Kit, I talk about how there are two of me, the softer side of me and the care giving side of me. The care giving side of me knows what the softer side of me likes, so she takes care of us by doing things we like when the softer side of me feels down, lonely, sad, hurt, or disappointed (lol I know that sounds bipolar but it really isn't). I like to cook; it is what relaxes me. So I learned when I wanted to relax and unwind, to cook or bake. I got into new music because music is what speaks to my soul. I learned the things that made me sad and the things that made me happy again. I learned what made me laugh and what made me cry. I learned how to recognize certain behaviors and the things that triggered them. I learned every possible thing I could about who I was, what I was, and why I was. The same effort that I would have given to a man and relationship if I had one, I learned how to put that into myself. And I eventually created my own personal sacred space around me that allowed me to enjoy being with me first! I did not need anyone to make me happy because I now knew how to do that for myself. I did not need to depend on someone else's love to feel valued and valuable because I did that for myself. And I did not need anyone to affirm my worth because I was now able to affirm it for myself.

One of the major things I also discovered during this time of being single was what I wanted to spend my life doing. I always knew that I was not a 9-5 type gurl, but how I wanted to fill that time I was very unsure of. It wasn't until I figured out me I was then able to create the life I wanted for myself as far as my career. I discovered my passions and my purpose, and I began to organize them into a business. The amount of time that I spent on creating every aspect of my business would have been lost in a man had I been in a relationship. I wouldn't have been focused on building and fulfilling my dream career because I would have been focused on building my dream relationship. Not to say that you can't have both, but I am a firm believer that you can't put the same effort into both at the same time. Both of them take work and I believe you have to tackle one before you can tack the other. Well, since I was single, I tackled my dream career first. And because of it, I am a better person that I can bring to the table. And I also believe I will attract the man I desire as well, someone who too is focused and passionate about what he chooses to do with his life.

There is something magnetic about this mind shift. If you really want to attract the companion that you desire, shift the focus on you being the absolute best person you can bring to the table. You'll be surprised how caught up you'll get into creating this space around you. It does not take the desire away. Like I mentioned earlier, I still have my desires. But it makes being single so much easier to manage while you are waiting for that magnetic attraction to manifest itself. And not to mention, a woman who is confident, secure, and has her stuff together are very sexy attributes!

For this first week we are going to take the journey of creating your personal sacred space and rediscovering who you really are. Your personal sacred space is simply your own personal space that you create for yourself and around yourself. It is deemed sacred because this is where you live with yourself 24/7, so it has to be viewed as the most valuable thing about you and that you carry with you. Because of the time you put into creating personal sacred space, it has to be treated with the upmost honor and respect. When you honor and respect this space, then you will not allow others to disrespect your space. That means you will not entertain mess because you realize that mess will disrupt the balance you have created within yourself and around yourself. This is probably the most important factor to being single and happy. Like the saying goes "I can do bad all by myself."

PUT IT ON A POST-IT

- Being single is an art because not everyone can be unmarried and unattached while at the same time maintaining their own happiness
- Being single and happy requires you to have to shift your views and perceptions of what being single really means
- There is something magnetic about this mind shift
- Personal sacred space is simply your own personal space that you create for yourself

THE INVESTMENT

Sacred space is the most important space you can be in. This is where you are free to be exactly who you are. This week we are going to focus on creating sacred space and recognizing who, what, and why you are.

Directions: Each day fill in the blanks to each question. Track your daily progress in your Be Beautiful Journal component by going through your day, recording your actions, your emotions, your thoughts, your challenges, and how you managed the overall process

DAY 1

What do you like having around you to make you feel good? For me it is things like candles, music, any form of water (from the beach to the electronic waterfall), the scented wax warmer for smell, and good scenery (from the cabin in the woods to paintings, and flowers on the table). List at least 4 things that you can put around you to make you feel good.

1. _____

2. _____

3. _____

4. _____

Where can you place these things in your home so you can have a place of escape and refuge for yourself? For me it is in my kitchen and in my bedroom.

1. _____

2. _____

Use the items you listed and create your sacred space in the room you chose in your home. I would limit the things you surround yourself with so you can avoid clutter, that will become overwhelming and defeat the purpose. Once you have established your space, spend at least 30 minutes a day there and be sure to take your *Be Beautiful* Journal component with you and write whatever comes to mind. Enjoy!

Day 2

Another component of sacred space is not only the space you create around you but the space you carry with you. This includes bringing yourself into harmony and balance within yourself by spending time with you and only you. Find 30 minutes to spend today in the space you have created. Use your *Be Beautiful* Journal component to write and reflect. Use the following questions as a guide, but you are encouraged to write whatever comes to your mind and is in your space.

When I sit alone in my sacred space today the first thing that comes to my mind is...

Something I am very proud of myself for is...

Something I know I can improve in my life is...

One thing that makes me happy is...

One thing I love about myself is...

One thing I am grateful for is...

Day 3

Sacred space includes bringing yourself into harmony and balance within yourself by spending time with you and only you. Spend 30 minutes today in the space you have created. Use your *Be Beautiful* Journal component to write and reflect. Use the following questions as a guide, but you are encouraged to write whatever comes to your mind and is in your spirit.

When I sit alone in my sacred space today the first thing that comes to my mind is...

Something I am very proud of myself for is...

Something I know I can improve in my life is...

One thing that makes me happy is...

One thing I love about myself is...

One thing I am grateful for is...

Day 4

Sacred space includes bringing yourself into harmony and balance within yourself by spending time with you and only you. Spend 30 minutes today in the space you have created. Use your *Be Beautiful* Journal component to write and reflect. Use the following questions as a guide, but you are encouraged to write whatever comes to your mind and is in your spirit.

When I sit alone in my sacred space today the first thing that comes to my mind is...

Something I am very proud of myself for is...

Something I know I can improve in my life is...

One thing that makes me happy is...

One thing I love about myself is...

One thing I am grateful for is...

Day 5

Sacred space includes bringing yourself into harmony and balance within yourself by spending time with you and only you. Spend 30 minutes today in the space you have created. Use your *Be Beautiful* Journal component to write and reflect. Use the following questions as a guide, but you are encouraged to write whatever comes to your mind and is in your spirit.

When I sit alone in my sacred space today the first thing that comes to my mind is...

Something I am very proud of myself for is...

Something I know I can improve in my life is...

One thing that makes me happy is...

One thing I love about myself is...

One thing I am grateful for is...

Day 6

Sacred space includes bringing yourself into harmony and balance within yourself by spending time with you and only you. Spend 30 minutes today in the space you have created. Use your *Be Beautiful* Journal component to write and reflect. Use the following questions as a guide, but you are encouraged to write whatever comes to your mind and is in your spirit.

When I sit alone in my sacred space today the first thing that comes to my mind is...

Something I am very proud of myself for is...

Something I know I can improve in my life is...

One thing that makes me happy is...

One thing I love about myself is...

One thing I am grateful for is...

Day 7

Sacred space includes bringing yourself into harmony and balance within yourself by spending time with you and only you. Spend 30 minutes today in the space you have created. Use your Be Beautiful Journal component to write and reflect. Use the following questions as a guide, but you are encouraged to write whatever comes to your mind and is in your spirit.

When I sit alone in my sacred space today the first thing that comes to my mind is...

Something I am very proud of myself for is...

Something I know I can improve in my life is...

One thing that makes me happy is...

One thing I love about myself is...

One thing I am grateful for is...

SELF-LOVE IS THE BEST LOVE

Life is always good when you treat yourself! Do a little something extra for yourself either today or tomorrow. When we treat ourselves first, then we teach ourselves how we would like to be treated by a mate as well. Choose below from the list of ways to romantically treat YOU! Or think of one of your own.

- ♥ Make yourself a special dinner you would normally make for a mate

- ♥ Draw yourself a bubble bath, light candles, and play your favorite music

- ♥ Buy yourself some flowers and display them somewhere in your home

- ♥ Leave yourself an appreciation note in the morning before you leave out to go to work/school, so you will come home to it in the evening.

- ♥ Take yourself on a date to your favorite place, yes by yourself!

I am a strong believer, for someone who desires to have a relationship, we find ourselves in this single status longer than what we would like because we make the same mistakes with each person we meet, date, or even enter into a relationship with. I can definitely say this has been one of my mistakes. Eventually, I always found myself right back to being single. The two most common mistakes I have not only made myself but see a lot of women make as well are moving too fast and being insecure. I think those two are synonymous with each other, with being insecure being the primary issue. When I was insecure I had a tendency to move the relationship along very quickly, including my feelings, because I was afraid of losing the person I was involved with. This fear can be rooted in a few different things: afraid of being alone, afraid of being hurt, the fear of them finding someone else, or even afraid of not getting what you want in the end.

Now, I know there is a saying "you can't help who you love," but actually, you can, especially when you reach a certain age in life. For me, because I can only speak for myself, love developed first in my head. I would day dream all of the things I liked about the person and even the times we spent together. I found myself falling in love with the idea of what I had mentally developed rather actually first knowing and understanding what love is, and then evaluating if this person was worth extending that to on a romantic level.

This was the primary reasons I found myself hurt and all discombobulated after each failed attempt to date someone or be in a relationship with someone. I became obsessed with the idea of someone and the idea of being with that person. I gave of myself, in a lot of different ways, too quickly. I wanted to do things for them like cook for them and man spoil them before I got to know who they are and if they were worth giving this part of myself to them. Because I was in love with the idea of them, I gave of myself sexually because, besides the hormone rage, for me this was another way I could express what I told myself I was feeling. I did all of these things without giving time for the relationship to develop and grow, and without giving myself the opportunity that I deserved to get to know the person I was desiring to connect myself to. I failed to give them the opportunity to get to know me and to pursue me. So I found myself in a cycle of unsuccessful attempts at dating and relationships all because I wasn't patient enough to allow things to develop at a healthy pace. If we slow those things down in our head and actually think things through, the success rate of either not being hurt or disappointed, or the success rate of a relationship, may actually be a lot greater than what you have previously experienced.

Now this isn't to say that those relationships where you meet someone, instantly connect, and 30 days later (or sometimes less) you're married aren't possible. They are, BUT they are very rare and the success rate of those relationships/marriages are rare as well. Getting to know someone first without rushing things first in your mind and second through your actions, are of much benefit to you, the other person, the relationship, and your heart!

Before I could change the way I dated or "relationshipped" I had to first recognize where I was going wrong, and then fix it. To fix it, I had to first be honest with myself and second ask myself the hard question of why. Why was I afraid of not getting what I wanted? Why was I afraid of being alone? Why was I afraid of him finding someone else? As I mentioned earlier, the answers to all of those questions boiled down to insecurity for me. So then I had to ask myself the question, "Why am I insecure?" Of course, this required a lot of soul searching and self-evaluating.

To answer this question, I was insecure because I didn't know myself and I had not done the work on myself to become who I truly wanted to be. I had nothing to live for in my life. I had not figured out my purpose quite yet, I had no straight career path, I didn't know me enough to love me enough to protect me enough, therefore I had no idea about honoring, who, what, and why I was through my relationships. I was entering into or desiring relationships for all of the wrong reasons and for none of the right reasons.

The next thing I had to do was forgive myself for all of the mistakes I made in my past relationships, and then forgive all of the men and people I felt wronged me, including my parents and their divorce (this one I still struggle with quite honestly). I had to let all of that anger, hurt, and disappointment go! It wasn't doing anything but weighing me down and preventing me from moving forward in a healthy way. I found that I was carrying all of this baggage with me from situation to situation and relationship to relationship. A lot of journaling helped me in this area. Everything I felt I wrote it down. If I needed to write a letter to someone cussing them out, I did it in the journal and never mailed it. Then I replaced all of those negative feelings I let out with positive thoughts and feelings. I printed words and phrases out on paper and posted them all around my house so that I was constantly refilling myself back up, but with positivity. This is important, whenever you remove something negative, remember to always replace it with something positive.

Believe it or not, all of the relationships we have with people affect each other. If we feel like we can't trust someone in one relationship (friendship, with a family member, with a coworker) then we are carrying pieces of that same mentality into our other relationships. It's something about that *one relationship* that has the possibility to make us suspicious of that *one action* in all of our other relationships. Not only that, but *we* tend to carry the same behaviors with us from one relationship to another. If you can't forgive in a friendship or with a family member, then you're going to have a hard time forgiving in a relationship. So learning and practicing forgiveness is crucial. It doesn't mean you *forget* their action, but you do release all of the negative feelings you have that are associated with their action(s).

Another thing that helped me in forgiving is to just see people for who they really are, accepting them as that person, and expecting them to be that person. That way there are no surprises. If I have learned that you are someone who is dishonest, I am not mad at you for being dishonest, I just know I can't always expect honesty from you when I talk to you or deal with you. Therefore, I hold conversations with you and only deal with you in a way that really does not hold too much weight. Your dishonesty will not hurt me and I do not have to be disappointed with you in the end.

The last thing I had to learn to do was change my definition of a relationship and the things I was looking to get out of one. I looked at a relationship as something that would rescue me from singleness, something that would rescue me from my insecurities, something that would rescue me from the negative perceptions of others, and even something that would rescue me financially. I was WRONG!! Boy was I wrong! These are all of the wrong reasons to want or get into a relationships. The only person that can rescue you is yourself, with the help and love of God. The only person that can deal with your insecurities is you, with the help and love of God. And the only person who can get you together financially is you, with the help and love of God.

Yes, the road may be rocky, bumpy, and a plain ole hard one to walk, but it is not impossible for you to be all that you need to yourself and for yourself! It's just going to take some work and releasing a lazy mindset. I have a desire that supersedes a physical connection with someone, I want a mental and spiritual connection with my companion. I want God's heart personified in my life.

Today my reasons for wanting a relationship and eventually marriage have changed. I love this life of my mine that I have created and am still creating so much I want to share it with a deserving man. While I am no longer afraid to be alone, ultimately, no, I don't want to be alone. I do want to build an extension of my life with someone. I think there is something unique about the growth that you experience as a person with a significant other. It is a different type of growth than the one you experience as an individual. I am open to that growth. There is nothing wrong with wanting a relationship because I believe we were created to commune with each other on various levels. The problem lies behind the unhealthy reasons for wanting to fulfill these desires.

When you want a relationship to fill a void in your life that is an unhealthy reason to want one. Just like I was looking for a relationship to fill the void of loneliness, insecurities, financial stability, and everything else in between, those were unhealthy reasons to want a relationship. I don't know how many times I can say this, don't **EVER** feel bad about wanting companionship, a relationship, a marriage, or being connected to your soul mate. There is absolutely nothing wrong with having those desires as a woman. It is when the reasons behind them are unhealthy, like needing or wanting to fill a void.

This week you will focus on identifying the reasons why you want a relationship and determining whether or not they are healthy. First, you will examine how you define relationships and their purpose. Next, you will identify exactly what you are looking to get out of your relationships. This is going to require you to really think things through and be honest with yourself so you can truly identify if these are healthy reasons. Lastly, you are going to identify the mistakes you have made and keep making that keep finding yourself in and out of unhealthy relationships. Have a great week of discovering yourself on another level!

PUT IT ON A POST-IT

- ♥ There is nothing wrong with you for wanting a relationship
- ♥ We find ourselves in this single status longer than what we would like because we make the same mistakes with each person we meet, date, or even enter into a relationship with
- ♥ Forgiveness is key! Only expect someone to be who they show you to be, nothing more
- ♥ If you are trying to fill a void through a relationship, it is an unhealthy reason to want a relationship
- ♥ Only you and God can fill your voids

THE INVESTMENT

Directions: Follow the instructions for each day. Track your daily progress in your *Be Beautiful* Journal component by going through your day, recording your actions, your emotions, your thoughts, your challenges, and how you managed the overall process. Use the feelings wheel in the Appendix for help with identifying your feelings.

Day 1

What does being in a relationship means to you? Give as much detail as possible. Include what role you see yourself playing in the relationship and what role you see your mate playing in a relationship.

_____

_____

_____

_____

_____

Do you think this is a healthy view of a relationship? Why or why not?

_____

_____

_____

_____

_____

Do you or have you ever had any healthy examples of relationships in your life? If so who's relationship? What was it about their relationship that made it healthy?

_____

_____

Do you or have you ever had any unhealthy examples of relationships in your life? If so, who's relationship? What was it about their relationship that made it unhealthy?

_____

_____

_____

_____

Do you notice yourself mimicking these unhealthy examples in your own relationships? If so, how?

_____

_____

_____

Day 2

Name the mistakes you have made in the past when it comes to your relationships. Be honest with yourself without being too hard on yourself. Sometimes it isn't always your fault, sometimes the other person just was not ready. So an example of being honest without being too hard on yourself may be you may have held on longer than you should have. This is meant to be helpful to you, not tear you down.

Identify three mistakes you have consistently made in your past relationships.

♥ _____

_____

_____

♥ _____

_____

_____

♥ _____

_____

_____

For each mistake you listed, how can you turn that into a learning lesson and do things differently the next time?

♥ _____
_____
_____
_____
_____

♥ _____
_____
_____
_____
_____

♥ _____
_____
_____
_____
_____

Single Is the New Sexxy   *Keedra A. Keeley*

Day 3

Today you will list all of the people you need to forgive and why. Be honest with yourself, this is the one place you can be totally honest about you and your life without facing any judgement. Use the *Be Beautiful* Journal component if you need more space.

Who do I need to forgive? What do I need to forgive them for?

♥ _____

_____

_____

♥ _____

_____

_____

♥ _____

_____

_____

♥ _____

_____

_____

Day 4

Name **one** reason why you want to be in a relationship. Identify whether this is a healthy reason or not. No one is reading this but you, so BE HONEST WITH YOURSELF.

One reason I desire a relationship is...

_____

_____

Is this a healthy or unhealthy reason? Why or why not?

_____

_____

Is this rescuing me from something I do not want to face on my own? If so what?

_____

_____

Can I rescue myself on my own? If so how?

_____

_____

Day 5

Name **one** reason why you want to be in a relationship. Identify whether this is a healthy reason or not. No one is reading this but you, so BE HONEST WITH YOURSELF.

One reason I desire a relationship is...

_____

_____

Is this a healthy or unhealthy reason? Why or why not?

_____

_____

Is this rescuing me from something I do not want to face on my own? If so what?

_____

_____

Can I rescue myself on my own? If so how?

_____

_____

Day 6

Name **one** reason why you want to be in a relationship. Identify whether this is a healthy reason or not. No one is reading this but you, so BE HONEST WITH YOURSELF.

One reason I desire a relationship is...

_____

_____

Is this a healthy or unhealthy reason? Why or why not?

_____

_____

Is this rescuing me from something I do not want to face on my own? If so what?

_____

_____

Can I rescue myself on my own? If so how?

_____

_____

Day 7

Name **one** reason why you want to be in a relationship. Identify whether this is a healthy reason or not. No one is reading this but you, so BE HONEST WITH YOURSELF.

One reason I desire a relationship is...

_____

_____

Is this a healthy or unhealthy reason? Why or why not?

_____

_____

Is this rescuing me from something I do not want to face on my own? If so what?

_____

_____

Can I rescue myself on my own? If so how?

_____

_____

SELF-LOVE IS THE BEST LOVE

Life is always good when you treat yourself! Do a little something extra for yourself either today or tomorrow. When we treat ourselves first, then we teach ourselves how we would like to be treated by a mate as well. Choose below from the list of ways to romantically treat YOU! Or think of one of your own.

- ♥ Make yourself a special dinner you would normally make for a mate

- ♥ Draw yourself a bubble bath, light candles, and play your favorite music

- ♥ Buy yourself some flowers and display them somewhere in your home

- ♥ Leave yourself an appreciation note in the morning before you leave out to go to work/school, so you will come home to it in the evening.

- ♥ Take yourself on a date to your favorite place, yes by yourself!

The last thing that any single woman wants to do is sit around waiting for the right one to show up. Gurl bye! That's not sexxy. There is always something we can be doing to better ourselves until our time comes for *that* one to show up in our lives. Believe it or not, you can actually get so busy and so focused on you, when your dream mate shows up, you won't even notice. They'll have to catch your attention so hard just to get you to look up and see them. I don't know about you, but baby do whatcha gotta do to get my attention honey! Cause I am focused on bettering me!

After I began to work through my issues and began figuring out why I was (my purpose in life), I was then able to focus on that. I went back to school and earned two master degrees, a Master's of Science in Organizational Leadership (MSOL) and a Masters of Divinity (M.Div). When I was living in Maryland I started a nonprofit organization called Speak Life, Inc. working with teenage girls in juvenile detention centers and offering them workshops on how to invest in bettering themselves before they reentered "the real world". From there, because I noticed the struggles their mothers were facing, I started a program in Speak Life called the Sistah Circle that worked to empower women. I also was a co-host on a Blog Talk radio show called I'm Every Woman on an internet radio station WXRP based out of Atlanta. It was during this time that became a pivotal moment in my life. When I was young my family lived in Atlanta, GA. I basically grew up in Atlanta. We moved there when I was seven years old and left when I was fourteen. Those are the most important years of a child's life as they form who that child will be. Because Atlanta had always felt like home to me (we moved around a lot until we settled in Atlanta), I always wanted to go back. It was while co-hosting on the blog talk radio station I finally made my decision to go back.

I was interviewing a cast member from the reality show Love and Hip Hop Atlanta on the blog talk radio show. I had so much fun doing it and afterward I thought to myself, "I need to be back down in Atlanta." It was then I made my decision to quit my government job, move back down to Atlanta, and pursue my dreams of living the life I wanted to live, not the life I felt like I had to live.

When I moved to Atlanta I started school, pursuing my second master's degree. Due to a few little issues I ran into with transferring Speak Life to Atlanta, I had to let that and the Sistah Circle go. Well, the legal side of it. But inside of me, I still wanted to work to empower women. So I prayed about what I should do and the best way to pursue my dreams. As I prayed God reminded me of all the things I had been through in my life and how other women struggle with the same things mentally, emotionally, spiritually, physically, and personally. So in May of 2014 Be Beautiful was conceived within me.

Over the next year, I took what God deposited within me and gave it life. It was not easy because I was also in school. So the process was a little slow. I also allowed myself to get distracted a few times, but because Be Beautiful was given to me by God, God always found a way to get me back on track.

Before I left Maryland I told myself I never wanted to work for someone ever again, and from this point on I was going to always employ myself because that was the life that I wanted to live. So I have stayed focused on creating the life I want to live so I do not have to go back to living the life I felt that I had to live. And now I am more focused than ever on building and maintain that for myself.

The desire for me to be in a relationship, or even get married, has not changed. But I am so focused on me and my life right now that it is not my one and only primary concern. I know there are greater and bigger things to life than being with a man or having a mate. And the wrong one cannot and will not have a chance to get anywhere significant in my life again because I am protective of all of the hard work I have done and continue to do on myself and my life.

When we shift our focus to bettering ourselves then the relationship and a mate we're waiting on are no longer our main focus or priority This even holds true if you have children. Now, I don't have children, so I am not suggesting you neglect them, but it is very important that you do not neglect yourself either. If you don't know how to be good to yourself, better yourself, and focus on yourself, then you will be no good to your children or to a mate. As my good friend, author of the *Audacity to Love* book series, D. Westfield would say "When you know your own value, you won't be so quick to give others a discount on your love."

I chose to focus on furthering my education and start a business, but that might not be the same for everyone. This week you will identify those things you are focused on and those things you could be focused on more than a relationship or a mate.

PUT IT ON A POST-IT

- When we shift our focus to bettering ourselves then the relationship and a mate we're waiting on are no longer our main focus or priority

- The last thing that any single woman wants to do is sit around waiting for the right one to show up

- There is always something you can be doing to better yourself until your time comes for that one to show up in your life

THE INVESTMENT

Directions: Follow the instructions for each day. By the end of this week, you should have seven new things to focus on. Track your daily progress in your *Be Beautiful* Journal component by going through your day, recording your actions, your emotions, your thoughts, your challenges, and how you managed the overall process.

Single Is the New Sexxy   Keedra A. Keeley

Day 1

Name one thing you spend most of your time thinking about.

_____

_____

How is this beneficial to your life?

_____

_____

If it is not beneficial, name one thing you can replace this thought with.

_____

_____

If it is beneficial, how can you change this thought into something you are actually doing or achieving?

_____

_____

_____

Day 2

Name one thing you spend most of your time thinking about.

_____

_____

How is this beneficial to your life?

_____

_____

If it is not beneficial, name one thing you can replace this thought with.

_____

_____

If it is beneficial, how can you change this thought into something you are actually doing or achieving?

_____

_____

_____

Day 3

Name one thing you spend most of your time thinking about.

_____

_____

How is this beneficial to your life?

_____

_____

If it is not beneficial, name one thing you can replace this thought with.

_____

_____

If it is beneficial, how can you change this thought into something you are actually doing or achieving?

_____

_____

_____

Day 4

Name one thing you spend most of your time thinking about.

_____

_____

How is this beneficial to your life?

_____

_____

If it is not beneficial, name one thing you can replace this thought with.

_____

_____

If it is beneficial, how can you change this thought into something you are actually doing or achieving?

_____

_____

_____

Day 5

Name one thing you spend most of your time thinking about.

_____

_____

How is this beneficial to your life?

_____

_____

If it is not beneficial, name one thing you can replace this thought with.

_____

_____

If it is beneficial, how can you change this thought into something you are actually doing or achieving?

_____

_____

Day 6

Name one thing you spend most of your time thinking about.

_____

_____

How is this beneficial to your life?

_____

_____

If it is not beneficial, name one thing you can replace this thought with.

_____

_____

If it is beneficial, how can you change this thought into something you are actually doing or achieving?

_____

_____

_____

Single Is the New Sexxy   Keedra A. Keeley

Day 7

Name one thing you spend most of your time thinking about.

_____

_____

How is this beneficial to your life?

_____

_____

If it is not beneficial, name one thing you can replace this thought with.

_____

_____

If it is beneficial, how can you change this thought into something you are actually doing or achieving?

_____

_____

_____

SELF-LOVE IS THE BEST LOVE

Life is always good when you treat yourself! Do a little something extra for yourself either today or tomorrow. When we treat ourselves first, then we teach ourselves how we would like to be treated by a mate as well. Choose below from the list of ways to romantically treat YOU! Or think of one of your own.

- ♥ Make yourself a special dinner you would normally make for a mate

- ♥ Draw yourself a bubble bath, light candles, and play your favorite music

- ♥ Buy yourself some flowers and display them somewhere in your home

- ♥ Leave yourself an appreciation note in the morning before you leave out to go to work/school, so you will come home to it in the evening.

- ♥ Take yourself on a date to your favorite place, yes by yourself!

I know a few people may have a problem with me combining praying and sexxy together, but let's just be honest, it really is sexxy to see someone we are interested in praying. It means they have a relationship with God, or a higher spiritual power, which in my book is really important and extremely attractive. So, yeah, a praying man or woman is very sexxy. Ladies, we can still be holy without being homely! I prefer to be sexxy!

About a month before I started writing this book, God spoke to me very clearly and told me to start waking up at 6am in the morning to pray. Because I already am used to creating my sacred space in my home, I began waking up at 5:45am, making a space at the table in kitchen, lighting candles to set a peaceful atmosphere, turning on my little portable waterfall to create tranquility, and tuning in to some soft gospel music to create harmony. I make a cup of peach ginger tea, sit down at my table with my journal, and I pray for an hour. This has now become a regular part of my day.

At the time, I had something specific in mind that I was praying for concerning my relationships, so every day I prayed for God's blessings in this area, for God to renew all minds, for God's favor, for God to cleanse all hearts, and for God to keep the promise that was made to me a few months back. After I started praying, things started shifting. At first things started shifting in what appeared to be a negative way. But what I later realized was that my prayers had been heard and accepted and that those things that were shifting weren't negative, instead things were clearing out and moving in place for my prayers to manifest themselves.

The next few weeks ended up being a very hard journey. A number of things started running through my mind. Even though I came to a realization about my prayers being heard and accepted, there were still days that I felt discouraged and had questions for God.

These questions were "Will God answer these prayers?" and "Does God even hear me?" and "Why don't I see God moving?" We've all been there. Praying but still left with questions and a sense of hopelessness.

It was during this time God showed me how to pray for the things I wanted in my life. It wasn't enough to just say this is what I wanted and then for it to be so. I had to do some actual spiritual work for it because let's face it, any relationship we enter in we want it to be a divinely appointed relationship from God and God alone. Not to say that the relationship will be perfect, but, when it is divinely appointed that means God has given God's blessing to it. Anything that God has blessed is sure to be of the best.

The biggest thing God has taught me is that this practice teaches you and prepares to be a wife, because ultimately when dating and in relationships, the goal is to be in a loving and committed God ordained union. If you're looking for anything less then, well, just go ahead and skip over this week and go on to the end of the book. But if you're really looking for something of meaning and of substance, then this is actually where it all begins. Don't wait until God sends your spouse to start praying, now is the perfect time. God will shape you and mold you into the wife God wants you to be, all through teaching you how to pray.

The most important thing you can do is pray for your relationship and for your spouse. There are certain things you have to pray for in each stage to assure God is sending the right person to you and that you are the right person for them as well. There are certain things that need to be prayed to cover your mind, your heart, your spirit, and your body, in addition to covering your spouse's mind, heart, spirit, and body. This is where real wives are made and where lasting relationships and marriages are developed and maintained. All through prayer.

Now I'll be totally honest and transparent, before I started praying regularly and faithfully with a purpose, I was spiritually weak, and that affected everything about me. Flat out, I was a wimp. I would cry over everything that didn't go the way I had hoped when it came to my relationships. I was always walking around feeling defeated on the inside. I walked around feeling sad and wondering if I was ever going to get the love I saw others with. Don't get me wrong, I know how to be single, and at certain times I do very much enjoy being single, I love myself! I have done much work on myself to get to know myself, to love myself, to build up confidence in myself, to come to a healthy place within myself, to be aware of myself, and to figure out life's purpose for myself. But, there are times in your singleness when you do want everything that comes with companionship, and those times do get difficult. Hey! I'm human! But what I have also come to learn and appreciate is that I don't want companionship with just anyone, I want it with the right person that God has ordained for me. So for that I can be patient enough and continue to pray God works that out for me. And God already is by teaching how to be the best wife, best friend, best companion, best spouse, and best prayer partner I can possibly be to a more than deserving man.

This week we are going to get the process started of praying for the right person to come into your life and for the wrong one's to exit stage right. We are going to cover ourselves in prayer first so that we are praying those things that God wants us to pray for. And then we are going to speak some things into existence and pray for the strength to endure this waiting period. I will be honest with you, when you start to pray and you pray with a faithful and earnest heart, it is going to get challenging. But I speak from experience when is say don't give up; your prayers are being heard and being acknowledged.

And in order to endure a marriage, you have to first learn how to fight for it through prayer.

(To learn more about how prayer works, the power of prayer, and how to pray, self-invest in the *Be Beautiful Spiritually* workbooks)

PUT IT ON A POST-IT

- We all have those times where we question if God hears our prayers or where God is. It's normal. Keep praying
- Prayer is where I learn and prepare how to be a wife
- The most important thing I can do is pray for my future relationship and my future spouse
- There are certain things I have to pray for in each stage to assure God is sending the right person to me and that I am the right person for them as well
- Allow God to teach me how to be the best friend, the best wife, the best companion, and the best prayer partner

THE INVESTMENT

Directions: Each day this week, find something you can pray about for yourself and for your desired mate. Write your prayers out in your *Be Beautiful* Journal component. There is something about seeing the prayers you pray written out that helps make them more real to you. Track your daily progress in your *Be Beautiful* Journal component by going through your day, recording your actions, your emotions, your thoughts, your challenges, and how you managed the overall process. Use the Feelings Inventory Wheel in the Appendix for help with identifying your feelings.

Example:

Today for myself I pray....

> *That I begin speaking to others with kind and uplifting words instead of words that are filled with judgement and anger*

Today for my desired mate I pray....

> *That love fills their heart so much so it becomes a reflection of God's love toward me*

Single Is the New Sexxy   Keedra A. Keeley

Day 1

Today for myself I pray....

_____
_____
_____
_____
_____
_____
_____
_____

Today for my desired mate I pray....

_____
_____
_____
_____
_____
_____
_____
_____

Day 2

Today for myself I pray....

Today for my desired mate I pray....

Day 3

Today for myself I pray....

Today for my desired mate I pray....

Day 4

Today for myself I pray....

_____
_____
_____
_____
_____
_____
_____

Today for my desired mate I pray....

_____
_____
_____
_____
_____
_____
_____

Day 5

Today for myself I pray....

_____

_____

_____

_____

_____

_____

_____

_____

Today for my desired mate I pray....

_____

_____

_____

_____

_____

_____

_____

_____

Day 6

Today for myself I pray....

_____
_____
_____
_____
_____
_____
_____
_____

Today for my desired mate I pray....

_____
_____
_____
_____
_____
_____
_____
_____

Day 7

Today for myself I pray....

_____
_____
_____
_____
_____
_____
_____
_____

Today for my desired mate I pray....

_____
_____
_____
_____
_____
_____
_____
_____

SELF-LOVE IS THE BEST LOVE

Life is always good when you treat yourself! Do a little something extra for yourself either today or tomorrow. When we treat ourselves first, then we teach ourselves how we would like to be treated by a mate as well. Choose below from the list of ways to romantically treat YOU! Or think of one of your own.

- ♥ Make yourself a special dinner you would normally make for a mate

- ♥ Draw yourself a bubble bath, light candles, and play your favorite music

- ♥ Buy yourself some flowers and display them somewhere in your home

- ♥ Leave yourself an appreciation note in the morning before you leave out to go to work/school, so you will come home to it in the evening.

- ♥ Take yourself on a date to your favorite place, yes by yourself!

I have never been the woman to accept just anything from a man. I do have standards. I do not deal with cheating, I do not overlook multiple women, I do not allow any man to call me a bitch, I do not allow any man to put his hands on me, I do expect for a man to be in a relationship with me and only me, I do expect a man's attention, I do expect a man to treat me like a lady because I carry myself as a lady, I do expect a man to respect me, I do expect a man to respect himself. I have morals and values, first as a creation of a deity much bigger than myself, second as a person, and lastly as a woman. I walk with confidence and self-esteem in every step and stride. I know the game, and I am not afraid to call a guy out on it when he's playing it. I love to cook for my man. And I love keeping my man satisfied. And I consider myself to be an attractive woman. So, why was it so hard to keep a relationship and find a man?

Despite all of these things, I became very insecure with myself. Actually, *because* of all of these things I became insecure with myself. I did not understand that all of these things were benefits to who I was and those things that made me stand out. I told myself and I allowed others to tell me that my standards were too high. Instead of allowing these things to prove my self-worth, I allowed them to misinform me and tell me I wasn't good enough. Why? Because some guys didn't want relationships with me. At least not the guys that I actually wanted relationships with. I remember crying because I really didn't understand why someone wouldn't want to be with a woman who was educated, was very ambitious, had morals and values, didn't allow a man to walk all over me, had a sense of humor, was fun to be around (at least I thought I was lol), and not only knew how to cook but liked doing it. These were the standards I set for myself because one, I thought these were all good and attractive qualities for a woman to have, and two I worked hard at bringing out the woman that was inside of me. So how could anyone, any man not appreciate that?

For the life of me I just couldn't and didn't understand, what was wrong with *me*? I started resenting myself for being who I was. I started to become angry with myself because there was something in me that would speak up and say something if I thought I was being treated wrong. I felt I was keeping myself from my own happiness.

What I failed to realize at that time was that I was what is called "wife material." I was the kind of woman that a man does marry. The problem was that the men I was choosing weren't ready to marry. They wanted to be free to be with whatever woman they wanted, whenever they wanted, and how often they wanted without having to worry about or answer to a woman. Simply put, the guys didn't want a commitment, and I just wasn't that type to entertain anything that wasn't going to progress and move forward. Yes, I understand that not all men are like this and think this way, but the men that I was choosing were. And the mistake I made in this was thinking I could change them and what they wanted.

Now my intent is not to male bash here. I love the men! I am speaking to the women who are successful, who have standards, who respect themselves, who are desiring a mate but are *still* single, and are thinking "What is wrong with me?" There are always things we can better about ourselves. Especially for strong women who are used to doing and *have* to do *everything* (and I do mean *everything*) their selves in absence of a man in their life. We tend to "forget" how to treat the men in our lives and sometimes end up finding ourselves emasculating him. This is just one example. I just want these women to know you can be every bit of the woman you are and reasonably desire all of the qualities that you do without forcing anything with anyone. The man who is ready and willing to accept all of these things about you will come to you, just have patience and keep the confidence in yourself.

Now, let's take a side bar and revisit the emasculation of a man for a second. Let's keep it all the way real ladies, we tend to let our mouths get the best of us. Especially when we don't respect a man, when we are strong and independent women, when he does not make as much money as *we think* he should, and when a man does not measure up to *what we think* he should. And if you keep it all the way real with yourself, this is the reason why some women still don't have a man when they want one. Ladies we have to learn how to use our words for uplifting and not for tearing down.

We also have to learn how to change our perspective when it comes to men. Of course, we have in our head what we want, and if a man actually does step to us in a way that we want, but does not meet our check list (physical, financial, career, etc.), then we have to look within ourselves and reevaluate that check list, or maybe just throw it out altogether. If you can't respect him because that checklist is more important, then maybe he's just not the one for you, or you for him.

I recently heard a story from my friend Stacye. Stacye has been waiting on her husband for a very long time. Stacye is very well established. She has educated herself, she has her own house, she owns the family business, and is raising her son. Stacye has always had a sense of morals and values about her because that is just how she was raised. So Stacye rarely, if ever, put up with any foolishness from men because she valued herself and knew her own strength and worth. After many years of praying and waiting for the right mate, out of the blue, Stacye was introduced to the man of her dreams. Nothing about their relationship had to be forced and now Stacye and her man are preparing to be married. This story gives me hope and it should give you some as well. You do not have to compromise who you are for the sake of having a relationship.

So ladies, please remember, while there is always room for change and improvement within ourselves, there is nothing wrong with you. Some men are just not ready to settle down. As fine as he may be, if he is not ready to settle down there is absolutely nothing you can do about that. Keep being you, keep being sexxy, and keep Being Beautiful!

The *Be Beautiful* Book Series (Vol 1)

Be Beautiful Mentally: Who Told You You Weren't Beautiful?

Be Beautiful Emotionally: Bag Lady

Be Beautiful Spiritually: 30 Days of Prayer, Devotion, and Meditation

Be Beautiful Physically: My Body, My Temple

Be Beautiful Personally: Single is the New Sexxy

APPENDIX

Feelings Chart

Sad
Bashful
Stupid
Miserable
Inadequate
Inferior
Apathetic
Guilty
Ashamed
Depressed
Lonely
Bored
Sleepy

Powerful
Faithful
Important
Hopeful
Appreciated
Respected
Proud
Cheerful
Satisfied
Valuable
Worthwhile
Intelligent
Confident

Scared
Rejected
Confused
Helpless
Submissive
Insecure
Anxious
Embarrassed
Foolish
Weak
Insignificant
Discouraged
Bewildered

Peaceful
Content
Thoughtful
Intimate
Loving
Trusting
Nurturing
Thankful
Sentimental
Serene
Responsive
Relaxed
Pensive

Joyful
Excited
Sexxy
Energetic
Playful
Creative
Aware
Daring
Fascinating
Stimulating
Amused
Extravagant
Delightful

Mad
Critical
Hateful
Rage
Angry
Hostile
Hurt
Jealous
Selfish
Frustrated
Furious
Irritated
Skeptical

www.ingramcontent.com/pod-product-compliance
Lightning Source LLC
Chambersburg PA
CBHW042331150426
43194CB00001B/21